Handel

Wise Publications
London/New York/Paris/Sydney/
Copenhagen/Madrid

Exclusive Distributors:
Music Sales Limited
8/9 Frith Street, London W1V 5TZ, England.
Music Sales Pty Limited
120 Rothschild Avenue, Rosebery, NSW 2018, Australia.

This book © Copyright 1993 by
Wise Publications
Order No. AM91299
ISBN 0-7119-3539-4

Music processed by Interactive Sciences Limited, Gloucester
Book design by Hutton Staniford
Music arranged by Stephen Duro
Compiled by Peter Evans

Music Sales' complete catalogue lists thousands of titles and is free from your local music shop,
or direct from Music Sales Limited. Please send a cheque/postal order for £1.50 for postage to:
Music Sales Limited, Newmarket Road, Bury St. Edmunds, Suffolk IP33 3YB.

Your Guarantee of Quality
As publishers, we strive to produce every book to the highest commercial standards.

The music has been freshly engraved and the book has been carefully designed to minimise
awkward page turns and to make playing from it a real pleasure.

Particular care has been given to specifying acid-free, neutral-sized paper which has not been
chlorine bleached but produced with special regard for the environment. Throughout, the printing
and binding have been planned to ensure a sturdy, attractive publication which should give
years of enjoyment.

If your copy fails to meet our high standards, please inform us and we will gladly replace it.

Printed in the United Kingdom by
Halstan & Co Limited, Amersham, Buckinghamshire.

Air
from Water Music

Fairly slow

5

But Who May Abide
from Messiah

Moderately slow

Dance And Trio
from Amadigi de Gaula

9

He Shall Feed His Flock

from Messiah

Hornpipe
from Water Music

I Know That My Redeemer Liveth
from Messiah

How Beautiful Are The Feet

from Messiah

Moderately slow

Larghetto
from Concerto Grosso No. 12

Largo
from Xerxes

Lascia Ch'io Pianga
from Rinaldo

Let The Bright Seraphim

from Samson

March
from Scipione

Martial Movement
from Fireworks Music

Bright tempo

Minuet
from Berenice

35

O Lovely Peace
from Judas Maccabaeus

37

See The Conquering Hero Comes

from Judas Maccabaeus

Silent Worship
from Ptolomy

Where E'er You Walk
from Semele

Where Is This Stupendous Stranger

from Redemption

Themes from Hallelujah Chorus
from Messiah